**REAL WORLD ECONOMICS**™

# How
# Currency
# Devaluation
## Works

Barbara Gottfried Hollander

ROSEN
PUBLISHING®

New York

*This book is dedicated to my son, Joshua, a world traveler.*

Published in 2011 by The Rosen Publishing Group, Inc.
29 East 21st Street, New York, NY 10010

**Library of Congress Cataloging-in-Publication Data**

Hollander, Barbara, 1970–
How currency devaluation works / Barbara Hollander.
    p. cm.—(Real world economics)
Includes bibliographical references and index.
ISBN 978-1-4488-1270-7 (library binding)
1. Devaluation of currency—Juvenile literature. I. Title.
HG3852.H65 2010
332.4'142—dc22

                                                      2010009846

*Manufactured in the United States of America*

CPSIA Compliance Information: Batch #W11YA: For further information, contact Rosen Publishing, New York, New York, at 1-800-237-9932.

**On the cover:** Currency-exchange boards appear in banks in all major cities around the world.

# Contents

# INTRODUCTION

Money, or currency, can be found in countries around the world. People use money to buy goods such as homes, food, clothes, laptops, and cell phones. They also use it to pay for services, including going to a concert, a movie, or even to the doctor.

Most countries, or regions, have their own currencies. China uses the yuan, and Japan has the yen. The pound is the official currency in the United Kingdom, which includes England, Scotland, Northern Ireland, and Wales. Twenty-two countries, mainly in Europe, use the euro, which is a currency that began in 1999. But the most powerful and widely used currency in the world is the U.S. dollar.

Even though countries have different currencies, each kind of money has three jobs. First, money is a unit of account. It tells the value, or price, of a good or service. Second, money stores value. Money that is earned today can be spent today,

tomorrow, or years from now. Third, money is used as a medium of exchange. It can be traded for items that people demand, both at home and in other countries.

When people buy products or services from foreign countries, it involves converting, or exchanging, one country's currency into another. For example, the Nintendo Wii, Sony digital camera, and Samsung and Nokia cell phones are popular items in America. They are also goods made in other countries. Paying for goods from other countries involves exchanging currencies.

People who buy the Nintendo Wii in America will use U.S. dollars. But to bring these games from China, Americans first had to pay the Chinese. To figure out the amount that America owed China, both countries needed to know the exchange rate. They had to know how much of one currency was equal to a unit of the other currency. In other words, how many dollars were equal to one yuan?

There are more than 150 different currencies in use today. They come in different sizes, colors, and designs. The U.S. dollar is the most widely used currency in the world.

Some exchange rates stay the same. This means the amount of currency it takes to equal another currency is always the same. Before 2005, the exchange rate between the U.S. dollar and the yuan was fixed. But many exchange rates change. So the price of a product depends on the exchange rate at the time an item is bought.

A country watches its currency's exchange rates very carefully because they're connected to its economy. An economy involves making, selling, and buying goods and services. Countries want their economies to grow because this means people are working and companies are selling their products and growing bigger.

Sometimes countries even change the value of their currency on purpose because their government can no longer afford to keep the fixed rates. For example, when there is too much pressure on a currency's value to fall, a country may lower the value of its currency on purpose. This is called currency devaluation. In the past fifty years, many countries have devalued their currencies.

## CHAPTER ONE

# WHAT IS CURRENCY DEVALUATION?

Exchange rates are useful to people who travel to other countries. When visiting another country, hotels, cabs, restaurants, and even souvenirs will be priced in the foreign country's currency. For example, a hotel room in London will be priced in pounds. The U.S. dollar is so widely accepted that even in some foreign countries, it can be used to make local purchases. In the South American country of Ecuador, the U.S. dollar is actually the official currency.

## KNOWING THE RATES

Travelers use exchange rates to figure out prices, or how much things cost. For example, if someone from Italy travels to New York City, he or she needs to know the exchange rate between the U.S. dollar and the currency of Italy, known as the euro. Let's suppose the rate was one U.S. dollar equals 0.70 euros. This means one U.S. dollar can be exchanged, or traded, for

Currencies are bought and sold every day. When a person wants to exchange U.S. dollars for euros, he or she is selling U.S. dollars and buying euros.

0.70 euros. It also means a hotel room in NYC that costs $250 also costs 175 euros.

Many businesses also need to know exchange rates because they use them to figure out costs and make money. Businesses make profits by earning more money than it costs to make their products. Some businesses buy items from other countries to sell. Other companies use foreign products to make their goods. These businesses use exchange rates to help them figure out their total costs.

The United States and Canada both have currencies called dollars. Many other countries also use dollars, such as Australia and Jamaica. But just because all of these currencies have the same name does not mean they have the same value. In fact on December 26, 2009, one U.S. dollar equaled about eighty-nine Jamaican dollars.

# FLOATING RATES

The exchange rate between the U.S. dollar and the euro is an example of a floating, or flexible, rate. These kinds of rates change often—even several times in a second. In the previous example, one U.S. dollar could be traded for 0.70 euros. Now what happens if the exchange rate changes and one U.S. dollar equals one euro? This means the NYC hotel room that cost $250 now costs 250 euros. Since it takes more euros to equal one dollar, the euro has weakened, or depreciated, compared to the dollar. The dollar has strengthened, or appreciated, compared to the euro. Depreciation and appreciation describe the way floating exchange rates change over time.

# SUPPLY AND DEMAND

In a floating exchange rate system, the value of money changes because of supply and demand. Supply and demand are two important economic ideas. When someone goes to a store to buy a new cell phone, it is all about supply and demand. Supply and demand describes how buyers and sellers behave at different prices. Supply is the amount of cell phones the store will try to sell at different price levels. The demand is the amount of cell phones people will buy at different price levels.

Currencies also have supply and demand. Money supply is the amount of money in the economy. The cash in a person's wallet and the money in some bank accounts are part of the money supply. Most countries have a main bank called the central bank that controls the money supply. A central bank can take money out of the economy. It can also put more money into the economy. Changing the money supply affects how easy or hard it is to borrow money.

Demand for a country's currency depends on many factors. Think about that cell phone again. People may choose a cell phone based on price, features (such as touch screen), plans (unlimited texting), appearance (color, size), and even the reputation of the company that makes it. So demand depends on preference, or taste, confidence in the product, and most of all, price.

The demand for currency depends on these things, too—only in a bigger way. Currency is demanded by people who spend it to buy goods and services. People can buys things in their own country. They can also buy things from other countries. Products bought from foreign countries are called imports. Products sold to other countries are called exports.

When people in the United Kingdom demand American computers, the United States exports these goods to that country. The United Kingdom then imports the computers. How do imports and exports affect currency demand? Trade affects currency demand because countries use foreign currency to pay for imports or receive payments for exports. For example, when the United Kingdom buys American computers, it involves U.S. dollars and British pounds. It also involves the exchange rate between these two countries.

More than 90 percent of foreign trade is done by the shipping industry. By 2008, airplanes were carrying 40 million tons of freight a year, reported CNN. Ships carried 6 billion tons.

Confidence in the economy can also affect demand. This confidence is about people believing that a country's economy is going to grow. A strong economy backs up a country's currency. If people have confidence in a country's future

economic growth, they will demand more of its currency. But when something happens that causes people to doubt a country's economy, people will demand less of that currency. If people think they won't be able to buy as many things from that country, or if loans from that country won't be repaid, they lose confidence in that country's money. For example, in 2006, the United Kingdom arrested twenty-four people accused of trying to blow up airplanes traveling between London and the United States. Fearing the economic effects of another possible attack, the demand for the pound dropped.

Finally, there is something else that affects currency demand—interest rates. Interest rates represent the cost of borrowing money, such as taking out a loan. They also represent the amount of money earned by the lender, or the place that is loaning the money. Interest is earned on investments. An investment is something that people put their money into in hopes of earning more money. Higher interest rates earn more money on investments.

Governments can earn interest by lending money to other countries. Many countries spend more money than they have. For example, China and Japan have lent trillions of dollars to the United States to pay for overspending by the American government. In exchange for lending money, these Asian countries receive interest payments. When the U.S. central bank raises or lowers interest rates, it affects the money earned by these countries. So changes in interest rates also affect the demand for currency.

## Foreign Exchange Market

A stock market is a place where stocks, or ownerships in a company, are bought and sold. Stock exchanges are open for business during certain hours and days of the week. But there is a kind of exchange that runs around the world, twenty-four hours a day, seven days a week. It is called the foreign exchange market, and it is a place where investors buy and sell currencies.

Businesses trade currencies on the foreign exchange market, which affects the supply and demand for currencies nonstop. Just like with stocks, currency traders hope to make money when the value of the currency goes up. So traders buy currencies today that they think will be worth more in the future. Then they can sell the currency later and make money. The U.S. dollar is involved in 90 percent of all trades on the foreign exchange market, which trades more than $3.2 trillion each day. That's more than twenty-four times the dollar amount of goods and services made in the United States in 2008.

# FIXED RATES

Some exchange rates are fixed, or remain the same. For example, Hong Kong has fixed, or pegged, its currency to the U.S. dollar. So a certain amount of Hong Kong money will always equal the same number of U.S. dollars. Fixed rates make it easy for travelers to know how much things cost because exchange rates stay the same day after day. They also make it easier for businesses to know their costs and plan for

The Chinese currency has two names: the renminbi and the yuan. On May 11, 2010, one U.S. dollar could be exchanged for 6.8 yuan.

future production. These are advantages, or benefits, of a fixed rate system.

## FIXED RATE CHALLENGE

There are also challenges to fixed exchange rates—mainly, trying to keep them fixed. Remember the supply and demand pressures for a country's currency? They still exist in a fixed exchange rate system. Only now, the government and the central bank have to work hard to keep the rates fixed, even when both supply and demand are pushing the rates to change.

For example, what happens when more and more Americans demand Nintendo Wii games and other video games made in China? As Americans demand more games, the demand for the Chinese currency, the yuan, goes up. This puts pressure on the yuan to appreciate, or get stronger compared to the dollar. But if China wants to keep a fixed rate between the dollar and the yuan, it has to do something to offset the effects of the increase in demand. If it cannot offset these pressures, China has to lower the value of its currency on purpose. This is called currency devaluation.

## Gold Standard

Before World War I, many countries, including the United States and England, linked the value of their currencies to gold at a fixed exchange rate. People could actually take their money to the bank and exchange it for gold. The idea behind the gold standard was that money had value because it was backed up by gold.

But the gold standard created many problems because it limited the amount of money that could be put into the economy. If too much money was put into the economy, a country did not have enough gold to back it up. This would lower the value of the country's money. During World War I, countries put a lot of money into their economies to pay for the war. This lowered the value of their currencies and eventually ended the gold standard.

After World War I, countries tried the gold standard again. But terrible economic problems, such as economies not growing, ended this gold standard, too. Finally, after World War II, the Bretton Woods system was created. This system linked the currencies of major countries to the U.S. dollar and linked the U.S. dollar to gold.

Bretton Woods was around for more than twenty years. During this time, the American dollar became the world currency. It was used by people in different countries to buy goods and services. It was also used by countries for trading. For example, Asian countries (except for Japan) like China and Thailand traded with each other in dollars.

But by 1971, there were three times as many dollars held by foreign countries as there was gold in the United States. This meant that if these countries ever wanted to trade their dollars for gold all at once, the United States would not have had enough gold. In 1973, Bretton Woods ended and the U.S. dollar was no longer tied to gold. If the dollar is no longer backed by gold, what backs it now? It is backed by people believing the American economy will remain productive and the government will be able to pay its debts. This belief is so strong that the U.S. dollar is still the world currency.

17

## CURRENCY DEVALUATION

Currency devaluation is when a country lowers the value of its currency on purpose. Countries that have fixed rates often

At foreign exchange brokerages, brokers buy and sell currencies in response to changes in the market. A currency's value can change many times in a second.

devalue their currencies when they can no longer keep the pegged rates. Currency devaluation means the government changes the peg to one that makes the country's currency worth less compared to the currency of other countries. For example, in 1994,

Mexico devalued its currency, the peso. Before the devaluation, one U.S. dollar equaled three pesos. After the devaluation, one dollar equaled 3.4 pesos. Devaluing the peso meant it took more pesos to equal one dollar.

Sometimes with floating rates, governments and central banks still step in to affect their currency values compared to other countries. This type of exchange rate system is called a managed or dirty float. The value of the U.S. dollar is often compared to a basket of currencies, including the euro, the Japanese yen, the British pound, the Canadian dollar, the Swiss franc, and the Swedish krona. This is known as the U.S. Dollar Index. In the past fifty years, the United States has stepped in, or intervened, to raise or lower the value of the dollar, compared to these currencies, especially the euro and the yen.

## CHAPTER TWO

# CAUSES OF CURRENCY DEVALUATION

The exchange rate is usually determined by the relationship between money supply and money demand. However, this is not the case with a fixed exchange rate. When a government or central bank can no longer afford to keep the fixed exchange rate that it prefers, it may be forced to devalue its currency. Sometimes with a managed floating exchange rate system, a country may also devalue its currency against its trading partners. Many factors can cause a government to devalue the currency, but it all comes back to supply and demand.

## KEEPING THE RATE

One can think of a change in currency value like this: at first, one dollar is equal to ninety-two yen. Then the dollar weakens compared to the yen, and it takes two dollars to equal ninety-two yen. When the dollar weakens, it takes more dollars to equal the same amount of yen.

# Inflation and Currency Devaluation

Central banks try to help the economy grow by putting more money into the economy. They hope that people will use this money to increase their spending and that companies will use this money to expand into bigger businesses. But putting more money into the economy makes the money worth less. It also makes the prices of goods and services more expensive.

A rise in the general price level of commonly used goods and services, such as food, gas, and doctor's visits, is called inflation. Inflation can lower the demand for a currency in two ways. First, investors do not have a lot of confidence in countries with high or growing inflation. This lowers the demand for this country's currency.

Second, if inflation is high compared to interest rates, foreign investors will not want to invest in the country because they will not earn money. For example, at the end of the 1970s, the U.S. government was offering 11 percent interest to foreign investors. But inflation was 13 percent. Even though the investors could increase the amount of American dollars they had by 11 percent, the prices of things they could buy with the money rose 13 percent. So a foreign country that invested in the United States would have lost 2 percent. Since investors want to make money, not lose it, foreign investors stopped putting their money into U.S. investments, and the value of the dollar fell.

With floating exchange rates, the dollar and the yen would just equal this new rate. But if the United States wanted to keep a fixed exchange rate, it would have to find a way to increase the value of the dollar so that one dollar would still equal ninety-two yen. If it could not do this, the United States would devalue the dollar and accept a new rate that reflects the weaker dollar. The main difference between fixed and floating exchange rates is that in a fixed exchange rate, the government or central bank affects the supply or demand of currency to push back against factors that make the exchange rate rise or fall. What factors push a country's currency to fall? Basically, increasing the supply of money or decreasing its demand.

## Too Much Money

Increasing the money supply means putting more money into the economy. Sometimes a central bank increases the money supply to help the economy grow or pay for government expenses. Usually when there is

22

more of an item, it costs less. Think about a rare baseball card, which is very valuable. What would happen if someone found boxes of the same card? The value of each card would drop because it is not so rare anymore. The same idea applies to

On February 9, 2008, finance ministers and central bank governors from the G7 countries (including the United States, Japan, the United Kingdom, and Canada) discussed promoting economic stability.

money. When a central bank puts more money into the economy, it lowers the money's value. That is because when the central bank puts too much money into the economy, or puts it in too quickly, prices can rise and cancel out the benefits of the increased money supply.

Money supply and interest rates are actually connected. When a central bank puts more money into the economy, it also lowers interest rates. Since there is more money available, it is easier for banks to make loans, and the interest rates fall. This causes fewer investors to put their money into this country, since they can earn more money (interest) in another country. More money and lower rates put pressure on a currency to fall.

## Not Enough Demand

Decreasing currency demand can cause a currency's value to drop. For example, if Americans demand fewer products from Japan, it puts pressure on the yen to fall. This is because when America imports Japanese products, it involves yen. The less products that America buys from

Japan, the less yen America needs. This decrease in the demand for the yen makes the yen's value fall.

Lower interest rates also put pressure on a currency to fall. This happens because interest is the money earned from some

In 2004, China became the leading exporter of information and communications technology goods. These products include computers, cell phones, cameras, and televisions.

investments. If interest rates in the United Kingdom fall compared to other countries, investors from around the world will stop making investments based in pounds because they can make more money by investing in other countries. This causes the value of the pound to fall.

Currencies face downward pressures. These pressures can come from less demand for goods and services. They can also come from putting more money into the economy, which also lowers interest rates. When faced with downward currency pressures, countries can devalue their currencies to levels that better reflect the supply and demand for that currency, especially when they can no longer keep their fixed rates.

## Dollar Demand from OPEC

There is a group of countries that use, or demand, the American dollar to pay for their exports: the Organization of Petroleum Exporting Countries (OPEC). OPEC has twelve member countries, including Saudi Arabia, Iran, Iraq, Kuwait, United Arab Emirates, Nigeria, and Venezuela. According to OPEC's Oil Market Report for June 2008, OPEC produced about 37 percent of the world's crude oil supply, or 86.6 million barrels a day.

Countries that import OPEC oil pay for it in U.S. dollars. For example, when China, Japan, Germany, South Korea, and France buy oil from OPEC, they all pay in U.S. dollars. America is the biggest importer of oil and pays for OPEC oil in U.S. dollars. Since there are millions of barrels of oil bought each day, there is a lot of demand for the U.S. dollar that comes just from oil exports. But when demand for oil decreases, it puts pressure on the dollar to fall.

# FOREIGN EXCHANGE RESERVES

Foreign exchange reserves are used to maintain fixed exchange rates. Sometimes when these reserves are low, it can force a country to devalue its currency. Foreign exchange reserves are kept at the central bank. They are assets held in foreign currency. An asset is something that has value. Cash is an asset. U.S. dollars held by Canada's central bank are part of Canada's foreign exchange reserves. Many countries hold most of their reserves in U.S. dollars.

When a central bank wants to affect exchange rates, it can use its foreign reserves. For example, let's say the United States wants to lower the value of the dollar compared to the yen. Then the U.S. central bank, called the Federal Reserve, would buy yen using U.S. dollars. This means the Federal Reserve buys yen, or demands more of it. More demand for the yen increases its value.

Where does the Federal Reserve put these extra yen? It adds them to its foreign exchange reserves. To pay for the yen, the Federal Reserve sells dollars. So the Federal Reserve puts more dollars into the world economy. Increasing the dollar supply makes its value go down. Selling dollars lowers the value of the U.S. dollar.

A central bank uses its reserves to affect its currency's value. If a country is trying to keep a fixed exchange rate, it uses foreign exchange reserves to offset market pressures. For example, South Korea had a fixed rate with the United States for sixteen years. If the Korean currency was pressured to rise compared to the dollar, South Korea had to use its reserves to maintain the fixed rate. But what if South Korea did not have enough

Hong Kong, Singapore, South Korea, and Taiwan were called the four "Asian Tigers" because their economies grew quickly and steadily from 1960 until the mid-1990s.

reserves to push its currency's value down? It would be forced to devalue.

This actually happened in the 1990s—and not just in South Korea. It all started in the 1980s and early 1990s, when the

28

economies of Asian countries, including South Korea, Thailand, the Philippines, Malaysia, and Singapore, began growing a lot. These countries had a game plan for economic growth: Keep the costs of making products low, sell a lot of products to other countries, earn money, and put this money back into investment and education.

Interest rates in these countries were also high compared to other places, like the United States, so many investors put money into these countries. But these Asian countries did not keep much money in reserves. When their economies started falling apart, they did not have enough reserves to protect their currencies. So these countries were forced to devalue.

## CHAPTER THREE

# GROWTH OF CURRENCY DEVALUATION

Countries often devalue their currencies when they cannot maintain their fixed rates, and foreign exchange reserves are too low to keep the currencies' values. But there is another group of people who affect the supply of currencies in the world economy—foreign currency traders.

Currency traders buy and sell foreign currencies on the foreign exchange market. They make decisions that affect millions of dollars, or even more, each day. These traders have played a role in getting countries to devalue their currencies, and they can make currency devaluation even greater. Traders work for businesses that deal in foreign currency trading.

## SPECULATION

Speculations is all about what people guess, or speculate, might happen in the future. What if a person could travel to the future and learn the winning lottery numbers? He or she could travel back in time, buy a ticket with the winning numbers, and win

Currency traders in different countries buy and sell currencies. At any time of the day or night, there is a currency market open somewhere in the world.

$1 million. In real life, people cannot do this. But they can make the best, most educated guesses about what will happen.

Currency traders, also called speculators, make guesses about the future values of currencies all the time. Then they use this information to make money. Here's how it works: if a currency trader believes the value of the U.S. dollar will go up (or appreciate) compared to another currency like the British pound, the trader will buy U.S. dollars using pounds now. Then the trader will wait until the value of the dollar goes up and sell his or her dollars. Because the trader is selling dollars at a higher price than he or she paid, the trader ends up with more pounds than he or she had before.

How do traders choose which currencies to buy or sell? They compare a country's economy to its major trading partners, or the countries that trade with each other most often. For example, traders may compare the United States to Canada, China, Mexico, Japan, Germany, the United Kingdom, South Korea, France, Taiwan, and Brazil. Speculators compare countries by answering the following questions:

**Is a country spending more money than it has?** A government takes in money called revenue. It also spends money on expenses. When expenses are more than revenue, a country has a budget deficit. Many countries overspend, or run deficits. Traders usually see overspending as a bad sign for a currency—something that can lower its value.

**What is a country's trade balance?** A trade balance is exports minus imports. If a country is selling more products to foreign countries than it is buying from them, a country has a trade surplus. Exports are more than imports. But if a country is selling less products to foreign countries than it is buying from them, it has a trade deficit. Imports are more than exports. A trade surplus is seen as a good sign, or a reason for traders to buy a currency. But a trade deficit is a reason for traders to want to sell, or at least be worried, about a currency's value.

**How does a country's interest rate compare to the interest rates of foreign countries?** Interest is money earned from some investments, such as those offered by the government. If Germany offers higher interest rates than the United States, currency traders will see this as a good sign for the euro. To earn more interest, investors will demand more euros. Currency traders will buy euros so that they can sell them to investors looking to invest in German businesses and the euro's value will go up. If Germany lowers interest rates, investors won't want so many euros, and currency traders will focus on a different currency. In 2007, countries that used the euro did offer higher interest rates than the United States, and many investors bought euros and sold dollars.

Did you notice what speculators can do to a currency's value? They can make it even greater when the value is rising. They can make it even lower when the value is falling. Another way to say this is that currency traders magnify the change in a currency's value. For example, if the United States lowers its interest rates, foreign investors will soon demand fewer dollars. Expecting the dollar's value to fall, currency traders will rush to sell dollars, which pushes down the dollar's value even more.

## How America Rates

Currency traders look at government spending, trade, and interest rates to figure out which currencies to buy and sell. Spending responsibly, a trade surplus, and high interest rates can mean a strong currency. So how does America rate?

As of December 2009, the U.S. government had overspent more than $12 trillion. That's almost 85 percent of the amount of goods and services made in America in 2008. So the United States has a very big budget deficit. Additionally, according to the U.S. Census Bureau, the United States spent $32.9 billion more on imports than on exports in October 2009. So America has a trade deficit, too.

Finally, how do America's interest rates compare with other countries? In December 2009, U.S. rates were the same as those of Canada and Switzerland. But American interest rates were lower than the European Central Bank and much lower than interest rates in Australia, China, and India. So America does not rate well according to the list of speculators' questions.

# Peg It

In the year 2000, more than one hundred countries had their currencies fixed, or pegged, to other currencies. For example, Bermuda, the Bahamas, Panama, Argentina, and Hong Kong all have their currencies pegged to the U.S. dollar. One Bahamian dollar always equals one U.S. dollar. About 7.8 Hong Kong dollars always equal one U.S. dollar. Often, central banks will buy and sell their country's currency to keep it within the fixed rate.

# Protecting Your Currency

Many countries have abandoned the pegged exchange rate system and devalued their currencies. These countries include Mexico in 1994, Southeast Asian countries in 1997, Russia in 1998, and Brazil in 1999. One of the most famous cases was the U.K. devaluation in 1992. At this time, the pound was having trouble keeping its value in a pegged system called the European Exchange Rate Mechanism.

Most speculators did not believe the United Kingdom would try to raise the value of the pound. They believed the United Kingdom would leave the pegged system and devalue its currency. So speculators sold a lot of pounds, which pushed the pound's value down so far that it was removed from the pegged system on a day known as Black Wednesday.

Protecting a currency from falling can mean facing tough times. After the Bretton Woods system, the value of the U.S. dollar fell tremendously. To protect it from falling even more, Federal Reserve Chairman Paul Volcker put less money into the economy, which raised interest rates. This would help control inflation and make foreign investors buy American investments. Then the demand and value of the U.S. dollar would go up.

But less money and higher interest rates also meant banks did not have money to make loans. So people stopped borrowing, and businesses slowed their investing. Between 1981 and 1983, the economy shrunk by $570 billion. In 1982, twelve million Americans did not have jobs—the number of people living in New York City and Los Angeles combined. It was a high price to pay for protecting the dollar, but Volcker's move worked. Between 1980 and 1981, the dollar rose almost 35 percent compared to a group of other currencies, and inflation dropped.

But sometimes the fixed rate is set too high. In this case, market pressures keep pushing the currency's value down. Then the central bank tries to push the value back up by buying its own currency. If the government does not address the pressures

When people travel abroad, they can exchange their domestic currencies for the foreign country's currency. Money can be traded at banks, hotels, kiosks, and airports, among other places.

that made the currency fall, it can fall again. This pattern continues because the currency is overvalued. The government is trying to keep a value that is too high for the normal supply and demand conditions of the market. To stop this cycle, a country can devalue its currency compared to the pegged rate. This means it will set a new exchange rate that lowers the value of its currency. The government wants to pick a peg that will be less affected by the market pressures and easier to maintain.

There is also something called a semi-peg, or crawling peg, system. Instead of keeping one fixed rate, a currency in this system can have a value around a certain rate. So the currency's value may be a little bit more or slightly less than the fixed rate. A government can also change this band of rates often in response to changes in the economy, such as more inflation or higher interest rates.

Governments use crawling peg systems to devalue their currencies slowly and in steps, instead of all at once. For example, in the 1990s, Mexico wanted to devalue the peso compared to the dollar. It needed to devalue the peso a lot, but this would cause many problems in the Mexican economy. So it put in a crawling peg system and devalued its currency slowly. Mexico raised the band of rates in steps until the peso was devalued enough.

## Forcing Devaluation

There have been times when currency traders have pushed down the value of a currency so much that a country has had to abandon a pegged system and devalue its currency. This can happen when a country's economy is already weak—for example, if a

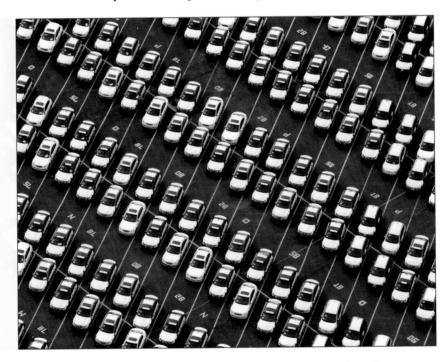

In 2009, the U.S. trade deficit grew because America bought more goods and services from other countries than it sold to them. Cars and oil were among the imported goods.

country is overspending and has a trade deficit, or if a country has high inflation and the economy is not growing.

Speculators see a weak economy as a reason to sell a country's currency. So they sell large amounts of the currency, which drives down its value a lot. The central bank then has to use its foreign exchange reserves to buy its own currency to keep the value from falling too much. Sometimes a country runs out of foreign exchange reserves and can no longer maintain its pegged rate.

Then the country is forced to get off the pegged exchange rate system and devalue its currency. In these cases, devaluation means a country has to fix its economy and try to gain back confidence in its currency. Professor David A. Leblang, of the University of Colorado's Department of Political Science, noted that speculators pushed emerging countries into forty-two devaluations from 1985 to 1998.

## CHAPTER FOUR

# EFFECTS OF CURRENCY DEVALUATION

Many countries devalue their currencies. A country may even prefer a low currency value because it gives it advantages. In the past twenty years, China has kept its currency from strengthening too much compared to the U.S. dollar. This has kept China's goods and services fairly inexpensive in the United States, which has helped China sell a lot of products to the United States. At other times, countries try to avoid devaluing their currency. A weak currency makes it hard for consumers to buy things that are made in other countries. Low exchange rates can also raise prices if businesses need to import materials from other countries. What would happen to China's exports if it devalued its currency?

## INCREASING EXPORTS

There is one major price difference between buyers from America and those from China who buy Chinese products.

China, currently the world's leading exporter, sells millions of dollars in exports to the United States each month. Many of China's exports are made of steel, including cars, screws, and steel pipes.

Buyers from America pay a price that is affected by the exchange rate between China and America. What happens if China devalued the yuan compared to the U.S. dollar? Currency devaluation would make Chinese products even less expensive in America. When a product becomes less expensive, more people buy it. So if China devalued its currency, Americans would buy more Chinese products. Chinese exports would go up.

How does currency devaluation make foreign goods less expensive? How does it increase total exports? Let's examine the effects of currency devaluation on Japanese exports. For example, if one U.S. dollar was equal to ninety-three Japanese yen, a Honda Accord automobile that costs 2,325,000 yen would also cost $25,000.

# The Current Account

A country keeps track of the money flowing in and out of its economy in the balance of international payments. The first section of this record is called the current account. The current account records exports and imports bought and sold during the year. Goods bought from other countries, such as cars, cell phones, and computers, are included. Services from other countries, such as shipping and insurance, also appear in the current account.

Sometimes people cannot find work in their own country. So they travel to other countries to find jobs. Often one person in the family will work in a foreign country and send the money home. This money is also counted in the current account. Governments record all trade and money transfers in the current account. Then they figure out their trade balances—and if they have trade deficits or trade surpluses. The current account also includes interest that foreign investors earn on domestic investments and that domestic investors earn on foreign investments. A country can use its current account information to see how important trade is to its economy. For example, are most of a country's products exported? For several European countries, including Hungary, the answer is yes. Hungary exports more than 75 percent of the goods and services it makes. In 1989, Hungary devalued its currency twice, which made exports more affordable and imports more expensive.

The other section of the balance of payments is called the financial account. The financial account is a record of investments by domestic and foreign investors. It keeps track of investments that foreign investors make in domestic businesses or in government investments. It also keeps track of which foreign investments domestic investors buy. So if a businessman in Japan buys shares in an American business, or if an American investor buys bonds from the Japanese government, these purchases would show up in the financial account for the United States. The interest they earned would show up in the current account.

The financial account always balances out with the current account. If you add up the financial account and the current account, the total is zero. That means when a country has a lot of imports and few exports, there are a lot of foreign investors helping domestic businesses grow. When a country has many exports and few imports, domestic investors are putting a lot of their money into foreign investments.

Now what happens if Japan devalues the yen and the new exchange rate becomes one U.S. dollar is equal to one hundred yen? That $25,000 car now costs only $23,250—that's $1,750 less after Japan devalued its currency. A lower price means more people will buy Honda Accords. More Japanese cars sold to the United States increases Japan's exports.

# DECREASING IMPORTS

Currency devaluation makes exports less expensive. As a result, more people buy them. It also makes imports more expensive, so less people buy them. This means goods and services bought from other countries now cost more money. In the yen-dollar example, American goods and services would cost more in Japan after the yen was devalued. When the price of a product goes up, people buy less of that product.

Let's say someone wanted to buy a new cell phone. The person went to the store and liked the latest Nokia phone, which is made in Finland. If currency devaluation made the U.S. dollar weaker than the currency in Finland (euros), the cell would be more expensive. For example, the exchange rate was $1 equal to 0.70 euros. So a phone that cost seventy euros also cost $100. Now let's say the United States devalued its currency and fifty cents equaled 0.70 euros. That phone would now cost $200.

Would the customer still buy the phone if the price doubled? Probably not—he or she would look for another phone that has similar features but costs less. Currency devaluation made the imported good more expensive. What about the cell phones made in America? Their prices stay the same, for now. If the customer found an American-made cell phone

By December 2001, Argentineans had suffered through a nearly four-year recession. Fearing that people would break into the store and take food, the Coto supermarket near Buenos Aires gave it away for free.

that still costs $100 and is similar to the Nokia phone, he or she would probably just buy that one. Often when imports become more expensive, people buy similar products that are made in their own countries. This increases the demand for domestic products.

## Better Trade Balance

Currency devaluation makes exports less expensive and imports more expensive. So more money flows into the economy and less money flows out. This makes the economy grow even more by improving the trade balance. A trade balance is exports minus imports. Countries, such as China and Japan, run trade surpluses. This means their exports are greater than their imports. Trade surpluses are good for increasing the size of a country's economy. Speculators also see them as a good sign for a country's currency.

Before 2002, the economy of Argentina was in trouble, with many people out of work and a trade deficit. In fact, exports were only 2 percent of all the goods and services made in the country. The government wanted to improve its trade balance and help its economy. So it decided to devalue Argentina's money, the peso.

Over the next few years, Argentinean exports rose. They became 7 percent of all goods and services made in the country. The government also put taxes on exports and earned money. Then it used this money to build up the country, including new roads. Argentina's economy was growing and more people were working. Currency devaluation helped Argentina improve its trade balance and its economy.

# Maintaining Foreign Exchange Reserves

Central banks hold foreign exchange reserves. A central bank can use these reserves to push down the value of its currency. Sometimes the central bank runs low on (or out of) its reserves. Then a country may be forced to borrow money from other countries to build them up.

Devaluation lowers the value of a currency so that a central bank does not have to use its reserves. It does not have to sell its currency to push down its value because the value is already lowered. Devaluation also gives a central bank the time to build up its reserves again. Countries with the highest foreign exchange reserves are China, Japan, Russia, Taiwan, India, South Korea, Hong Kong, and Brazil.

# Problems with Currency Devaluation

Currency devaluation can improve trade balances and result in more foreign exchange reserves. But currency devaluation also has some problems, including a loss of confidence and possible inflation. Many times, devaluations happen after a country has tried to push down its currency's value again and again, or when a country has deficits and is not growing. Both cases can make investors lose confidence in a country and not want to put their money into its investments. This leads to less money flowing into the country, which can slow economic growth.

Another problem with currency devaluation is inflation. Inflation is a rise in the general price level of commonly used goods and services, like food and clothes. Inflation means your

In the short run, currency devaluation can increase the demand for commonly used domestic goods, such as grocery products, and cause their prices to increase. This rise in prices is called inflation.

money cannot buy what it used to, because things are more expensive. For example, a dollar may have bought you a product at one time, but now it takes more than a dollar to buy the same item.

Countries don't want inflation for many reasons. At home, inflation means people can afford less. For the world, it means investors will not earn as much money and will lose confidence in that country's economy. This causes fewer foreign investments, which means less money is flowing into the country. Inflation is harmful to an economy. But what does currency devaluation have to do with inflation? It all comes back to demand.

Currency devaluation increases the price of imports. So a select group of goods and services becomes more expensive. Similar domestic products, or items made in one's home country, also become relatively less expensive. This increases the demand for domestic products. More demand for domestic products can drive up their prices, too. The rise in the prices of goods and services pushes inflation up.

# Ten Great Questions
## to Ask an Economist

1. Does currency devaluation make my money worth less?

2. What goods and services become more expensive after my money is devalued?

3. How does currency devaluation affect travel to other countries?

4. What does currency devaluation have to do with exchange rates?

5. Does currency devaluation affect the cost of studying abroad for a year?

6. Will currency devaluation raise the prices of products made at home?

7. If the country that I live in has a trade deficit, will the currency soon be devalued?

8. How is my country affected if one of its major trading partners devalues its currency?

9. How important are exports to my country's economic growth?

10. Can speculators force devaluations?

## CHAPTER FIVE

# DEALING WITH CURRENCY DEVALUATION

When a country devalues its currency, it can increase its exports and decrease its imports. This may lead to economic growth, with more people working and companies making more money. Countries also deal with the possible negative effects of currency devaluation, such as inflation. But there is something else a country has to deal with after it devalues its currency: the reactions of its trading partners.

## BETTER TRADE BALANCE EQUALS A GROWING ECONOMY

A country wants its economy to grow. This means people have jobs and are buying goods and services. Companies are selling their products and becoming even bigger businesses. More exports can help an economy grow. Some countries' economic growth depends on their exports. Currency devaluation leads to more exports.

In 2008, Japan's Toyota Motor Corp. became the world's largest automaker. Soon after, however, its worldwide rivals offered strong competition in the ever-changing auto market.

For example, when Americans buy Japanese cars, Japanese businesses make money. They use this money to make their businesses grow even bigger by opening more stores or building more factories. They also hire more workers, who

earn money and buy more products. When people buy more products, Japanese businesses make more money and the economy continues to grow. So when Americans buy Japanese cars, it helps Japan's economy grow.

Fewer imports can also make an economy grow because people are buying domestic products instead. This still means more business for domestic companies. When the Nokia cell phone became more expensive, Americans bought a similar American-made phone. This switch to American products also leads to American companies earning more money. This money is then used to make bigger businesses, hire more workers, and keep the economy growing.

## Handling Inflation

Countries worry that devaluation leads to inflation. To deal with inflation, central banks often raise interest rates. But raising interest rates also puts less money into the economy. This

In 2009, many countries, such as Russia, still faced hard economic times. People who had once shopped in expensive grocery stores changed their spending habits to lower their cost of living.

means less spending and investing, which slows economic growth. Higher interest rates can also attract more investment, which increases the demand for a currency and puts pressure on the money to rise again.

How often does devaluation lead to inflation? Eduardo Borensztein and José De Gregorio studied forty-one currency devaluations in emerging countries and their effects on inflation. According to their research, inflation occurred after the countries devalued their currency, and the inflation reached its highest level twelve to eighteen months after the devaluation. Therefore, devaluation did lead to inflation. But then in most cases (except in Latin America), inflation returned to around the same levels as before the currency was devalued. So in general, inflation did not have a lasting effect.

Sometimes when a country devalues its currency, it has to devalue the currency more than once. For example, in December 2009, Russia devalued its currency, the ruble, seven times—including three times during the week of December 22. Russia tried to maintain its currency value during this time. It even spent $100 billion in foreign exchange reserves. But it finally had to lower the value of its currency.

# Picking Up the Pieces

When businesses go bankrupt, it means they are legally not able to pay back the money they borrowed. The country of Iceland actually went bankrupt in 2008. It was unable to pay back the money it owed to other countries. Its currency, the krona, also lost a lot of value.

How did this affect people and businesses in Iceland that borrowed money? It made some owe even more. At this time, 13 percent of people in Iceland borrowed money to pay for their homes and held these home loans in euros, Swiss francs, and Japanese yen. This meant they borrowed money in kronas to buy homes.

Then they converted the money they owed to another currency. When the krona lost a lot of its value compared to these other currencies, the people just owed more in foreign currencies. As for the businesses in Iceland, 70 percent of money that businesses borrowed was also held in foreign currencies. After the krona's value fell, they owed even more, too.

Eventually, a lower krona value helped the economy of Iceland. Exports increased by 11 percent in a year, which included metal and fish. A devalued krona also led to more people visiting Iceland. When the krona's value dropped compared to the euro and the yen, these currencies became stronger. So Europeans and Japanese who visited Iceland had more purchasing power—their euros and yens could buy even more than they could before.

# THE OPPOSITE OF DEVALUATION

When a country lowers the value of its currency on purpose, it is called devaluation. But when a country raises the value of its currency on purpose, it is called revaluation. In the 1980s, the United States did both.

After the gold standard, the U.S. dollar was no longer backed by gold and its value fell—by a lot. Federal Reserve Chairman Paul Volcker took some strong actions to help the U.S. dollar gain back some of its value. The bad news was that the U.S. economy was hit hard: There was no growth, and many people were out of work. The good news is that the dollar came back strong. But some countries thought it came back too strong.

So in September 1985, the United States, Japan, West Germany, France, and the United Kingdom met at the Plaza Hotel in New York City. These countries (also known as the Group of Five, or G5) decided to devalue the U.S. dollar compared to the yen and the mark (West Germany's currency at the time—today, Germany uses the euro). This plan was called the Plaza Accord. It said that over the next few weeks, the dollar would be devalued by 10 to 12 percent compared to the other currencies. Central banks spent $10 billion in foreign exchange reserves to do this.

The Plaza Accord worked too well. According to Craig Karmin in his book *Biography of the Dollar*, the dollar's value dropped by 38 percent compared to the mark and 42 percent compared to the yen by 1987. In fact, the dollar's value fell so much that economies around the world began to panic. So the G5 countries met again and came up with a new plan called the Louvre Accord. The Louvre Accord called for a rise in the value of the dollar, also known as a revaluation.

## COUNTRIES' REACTIONS

When a country lowers the value of its money, it helps its trade balance. Exports go up and imports go down, which causes

The Great Depression ended the second attempt at fixing a currency's value to gold. President Franklin D. Roosevelt abandoned this gold standard and allowed the U.S. dollar value to fall.

the economy to grow. But what about the country's trading partners? If China devalues the yuan, its exports to the United States go up. This helps China's economy. But what about the U.S. economy? Americans are now buying more imports, so this hurts the U.S. trade balance.

When one country devalues its currency only to make its exports go up, it can hurt the economies of its trading partners. Sometimes a country responds to devaluations by its trading partners by devaluing its own currency. This is called competitive devaluation. It is also an example of beggar thy neighbor. Beggar thy neighbor is an economic idea where one country's attempts to help its economy hurts another country.

In the 1930s, countries were suffering through a time known as the Great Depression. Economies were shrinking. Millions of people did not have jobs. Businesses closed, and banks failed. Countries turned to beggar-thy-neighbor actions to try and help their economies, including devaluing their currencies. But these actions only upset their trading partners, who responded by devaluing their currencies.

After World War II, forty-four countries met at Bretton Woods, New Hampshire, and made two new global economic institutions: the World Bank and the International Monetary Fund (IMF). Part of the job of these institutions is to make sure the beggar-thy-neighbor actions from the 1930s, including competitive currency devaluations, do not happen again. The charter of the IMF actually says countries should avoid "manipulating exchange rates . . . to gain an unfair competitive advantage over other members."

## CHAPTER SIX

# WILL COUNTRIES CONTINUE TO DEVALUE?

Many countries have used currency devaluation for many different reasons. In a fixed exchange rate system, a country often protects its currency's value by using foreign exchange reserves or by raising or lowering interest rates. If this doesn't succeed, the country may need to devalue its currency. This happened in Asia in the 1990s. In a floating exchange rate system, currencies appreciate and depreciate—that is, their values go up and down only because of changes in the supply of and demand for currencies. But with managed floats, governments and central banks let the exchange rate float most of the time but use foreign exchange reserves and interest rates to make certain adjustments.

## THE ASIAN CRISIS

In the 1990s, several Asian countries had pegged their currencies to the U.S. dollar. These countries included South Korea, Malaysia, the Philippines, Indonesia, Singapore, and Taiwan.

When speculators anticipate that a country will devalue its currency, they sell the currency. Then after the currency devaluation, speculators can buy back the currency at an even lower price. They sell high, buy low, and earn money.

This fixed exchange rate system kept the currencies steady, or stable. By 1995, the value of the U.S. dollar began to rise. Since many Asian currencies were fixed to the dollar, their values rose, too. This hurt their exports because they were more expensive. It also made their trade balances even worse. These other countries had also borrowed a lot of money, and the loans were in U.S. dollars. When the dollar's value rose, they owed even more money. To make things worse, the money had to be repaid very soon.

Countries rushed to devalue their currencies, but it was too late. Speculators saw that these countries' economies were in trouble. They started selling a lot of their currencies, beginning with Thailand. The Thai currency fell by 50 percent compared to the U.S. dollar. These Asian countries did not have enough foreign exchange reserves to protect their currencies, so some tried another approach. They raised interest rates to attract investors. More investments would mean higher demand for their currencies. Malaysia actually raised its overnight lending rate to 40 percent. But these actions did not help, and countries were forced to devalue.

South Korea, Thailand, and Indonesia borrowed billions of dollars from the IMF to save their economies. Several countries, including Thailand, Hong Kong, and South Korea, left the fixed exchange rate system. This crisis also spread to other countries, such as Russia and Brazil. In Brazil, the central bank spent billions of dollars trying to protect its currency and even raised interest rates to 50 percent. But following other economic troubles, Brazil still devalued its currency against the U.S. dollar in 1999. A mix of economic problems, low foreign exchange reserves, and speculators' actions forced these countries to devalue their currencies.

## LEARNING FROM CURRENCY DEVALUATION

After the Asian crisis, these countries learned some important lessons. With the help of the IMF, South Korea, Thailand, and Indonesia have taken steps to fix their economies, including working on plans to pay back the money they borrowed. They also built up their foreign exchange reserves—in fact, South Korea has one of the largest reserves in the world. Their actions have brought back confidence in their economies, and their currencies are keeping their values. Even their current account deficits have turned into trade surpluses.

In 1997, Japan devalued its currency against the U.S. dollar by 23 percent. But in 1998, the yen was still falling compared to the American dollar. Countries feared a falling yen might lead to another Asian crisis. The yen needed help, and the United States stepped in to do so. Both the Japanese central bank and the U.S. central bank bought yen, hoping to increase the value of the yen compared to the dollar. This meant these central banks were forcing the value of the dollar down and the value of the yen up. On that day, the yen did rise, by 5.2 percent. But even after the yen rose, the Japanese prime minister said Japan needed to improve its economy to help its currency.

## Promising Not to Devalue

In 2009, most countries were still in a global recession. Their economies were shrinking. People were out of work, businesses were closing, and banks were failing. There was also a credit crisis, which meant people and businesses could not even borrow money to help them through the tough times.

Currency devaluations could have possibly improved many countries' economies—especially China, Japan, and Germany. The Asian countries usually ran trade surpluses, and Germany's economic growth depended on its exports. During this recession, exports in China, Japan, and Germany fell, as they did in many other countries.

Some people believed countries would start competitive currency devaluations. First, a country would devalue its currency to help its economy. Then a trading partner would devalue its currency in response, and this cycle would continue. There were twenty countries that felt currency devaluation should be talked about before it turned into a competitive currency devaluation problem. These twenty countries, called the Group of 20 (or G20), included the United States, the United Kingdom, Canada, Japan, China, Russia, and India. The European Union is also part of the G20.

The G20 met in London, England, in April 2009 and agreed not to use currency devaluation as a way to help their economies. "Unless they want to face fierce criticism by the other nineteen countries, I think that all G20 nations will hold their pledge against competitive devaluation," says Kathy Lien, a foreign exchange currency expert.

In April 2009, the United States, the United Kingdom, Canada, Japan, China, Russia, India, the European Union, and other G20 members met in London, England, and discussed competitive currency devaluation.

# Conclusion

Currency devaluations can often happen when economies are in trouble. Countries with strong economies are not often forced to devalue their currencies. Spending responsibly, a good trade balance, and adequate foreign exchange reserves can mean a sound economy. These measures also help keep inflation under control and interest rates at levels that encourage spending and investing, while still attracting foreign investors. All these things instill confidence in a country's economy and help it grow.

But countries do not always behave this way. Governments, including the United States, overspend. Countries also run

Following the April 2009 G20 Summit, Dominique Strauss-Kahn, the chief of the International Monetary Fund, believed that the G20 members were committed to helping the world economy recover from the global recession.

trade deficits—such as the United States, Britain, India, Japan, Italy, Mexico, and Brazil. Economies experience inflation, and some places, like Zimbabwe in 2008, suffer from severe inflation that has made their currencies worthless. Since central banks use interest rates for domestic economic goals, they are not always at levels that attract foreign investors.

When countries have economic problems, speculators can sell large amounts of their currencies and push down their values. Countries can try to defend their currencies, but this does not often work. When a country is being forced to devalue, it is usually trying to keep an exchange rate that is too high for the economy to support. Too many economic problems exist to keep the fixed exchange rate—problems that were often years in the making.

Today, foreign exchange reserves are a very small part of all the currency in the world. So the roles of speculators and other investors are becoming more important to a currency's value. This means countries will need to make responsible economic decisions. It also means currency devaluation will still be used when a country cannot maintain its currency's value.

# MYTHS and FACTS

**MYTH** Whenever a currency's value falls, it is called currency devaluation.

**FACT** Currency devaluation refers to lowering the value of a currency on purpose. Most declines in the value of currencies are because of changes in the supply and demand for currencies. These falls are called depreciations.

**MYTH** When a country devalues its currency, it only affects its own economy.

**FACT** Currency devaluation affects many countries, including the country that devalued its money, its trading partners, and other countries that use that currency (for example, to make purchases or hold loans).

**MYTH** Interest rates are not related to currency devaluation.

**FACT** Interest rates affect the demand for currency and are used by a country to protect its currency. A country raises them hoping to keep the value of its currency from falling. If this does not work and there are not enough foreign exchange reserves, the country is forced to devalue.

# GLOSSARY

**central bank** The main bank in a country that controls the money supply, issues currency, and holds banks' reserves.

**confidence** The belief in something, free of doubt.

**currency** A medium representing value that is designed to be exchanged.

**deficit** The amount that expenses exceed revenues.

**demand** The amount of goods and services that consumers are willing to buy at a certain price.

**devaluation** The lowering of the value of a currency on purpose.

**export** A good or service sold to another country.

**fixed (or pegged) exchange rate** A currency system where a currency's value is kept constant compared to other currencies.

**floating (or flexible) exchange rate** A currency system where a currency's value is determined by market conditions (or supply and demand).

**foreign** Something that comes from another country.

**foreign exchange market** A place where investors buy and sell currencies.

**foreign exchange reserves** The assets held in foreign currency by the central bank.

**import** A good or service bought from another country.

**inflation** The rise in the general price level of commonly used goods and services.

**interest rate** The cost of borrowing money, or money earned from some investments, such as loans.

**investment** Something that people put their money into in hopes of earning more money.

**money supply** The amount of money in the economy.

**price** The cost of a good or service.

**revaluation** The raising of the value of a currency on purpose.

**speculator** Someone who takes a risk in order to make a gain.

**supply** The amount of a good or service provided at a certain price.

**trade** The buying and selling of goods and services; involving money.

**trade balance** Exports minus imports.

**trade deficit** An amount that imports exceed exports.

**trade surplus** An amount that exports exceed imports.

# FOR MORE INFORMATION

Bank of Canada
Public Information
234 Wellington Street
Ottawa, ON K1A 0G9
Canada
(613) 782-8111
Web site: http://www.bank-banque-canada.ca
The Bank of Canada is Canada's central bank. Its duties
include carrying out open-market operations. These
operations change the amount of money available in the
economy and affect interest rates. They also influence
currency supply and demand.

Bank for International Settlements (BIS)
Centralbahnplatz 2 CH-4002 Basel
Switzerland
Web site: http://www.bis.org
The BIS is an international organization that encourages
monetary and financial cooperation. It also facilitates
dialogues between central banks throughout the world and
serves as their bank.

Board of Governors of the Federal Reserve System
20th Street and Constitution Avenue NW

Washington, DC 20551
Web site: http://www.federalreserve.gov
The Federal Reserve is the United States' central bank. Its
    duties include carrying out open-market operations. The
    Federal Reserve System is divided into twelve districts.
    The Federal Reserve Bank of New York Web site has
    information on the foreign exchange market.

International Monetary Fund (IMF)
700 19th Street NW
Washington, DC 20431
(202) 623-7000
Web site: http://www.imf.org/external/index.htm
The IMF consists of 186 countries that work together to
    encourage monetary cooperation, facilitate international
    trade, and promote both financial stability and economic
    growth. Its first job was to keep track of exchange rates.
    Today, it provides many short-term loans to countries with
    economic problems.

Organisation for Economic Co-operation and Development
(OECD)
OECD Washington Center
2001 L Street NW, Suite 650
Washington, DC 20036-4922
Web site: http://www.oecd.org
Based in Paris, France, this organization consists of countries
    that are both democratic and market economies. It is
    dedicated to promoting economic growth, maintaining
    financial stability, and increasing world trade. The OECD's

Web site also provides information on different countries, including exchange rates shown in U.S. dollars.

The World Bank
1818 H Street NW
Washington, DC 20433
(202) 473-1000
The World Bank is made up of the International Bank of Reconstruction and Development (IBRD) and the International Development Association (IDA). It provides billions of dollars in loans every year to developing countries.

# WEB SITES

Due to the changing nature of Internet links, Rosen Publishing has developed an online list of Web sites related to the subject of this book. This site is updated regularly. Please use this link to access the list:

http://www.rosenlinks.com/rwe/hcdw

# FOR FURTHER READING

Archer, Michael Duane, and Jim L. Bickford. *Getting Started in Currency Trading: Winning in Today's Hottest Marketplace.* Hoboken, NJ: Wiley, 2005.

Bernstein, William J. *A Splendid Exchange: How Trade Shaped the World.* New York, NY: Atlantic Monthly Press, 2009.

Booker, Rob. *Adventures of a Currency Trader.* Hoboken, NJ: Wiley, 2007.

Burrell, Jamaine. *The Complete Guide to Currency Trading & Investing: How to Earn High Rates.* Ocala, FL: Atlantic Publishing Group, Inc., 2007.

Chen, James. *Essentials of Foreign Exchange Trading.* Hoboken, NJ: John Wiley & Sons, Inc., 2009.

Cheng, Grace. *7 Winning Strategies for Trading Forex: Real and Actionable Techniques for Profiting from the Currency Markets.* Hampshire, England: Harriman House, Ltd., 2007.

Dolan, Brian, and Mark Galant. *Currency Trading for Dummies.* Hoboken, NJ: Wiley, 2007.

Epstein, Lita, and Gary Tilkin. *The Complete Idiot's Guide to Foreign Currency Trading.* New York, NY: Penguin Group, 2007.

Horner, Raghee. *Forex on Five Hours a Week: How to Make Money Trading on Your Own Time.* Hoboken, NJ: John Wiley & Sons, Inc., 2010.

Levinson, Marc. *Guide to Financial Markets*. Princeton, NJ: Bloomberg Press, 2003.

Lewis, Nathan. *Gold: The Once and Future Money*. Hoboken, NJ: John Wiley & Sons, Inc., 2007.

Lien, Kathy. *Day Trading and Swing Trading the Currency Market: Technical and Fundamental Strategies to Profit from Market Moves*. Hoboken, NJ: John Wiley & Sons, Inc., 2009.

Luca, Cornelius. *Trading in the Global Currency Markets*. New York, NY: Prentice Hall Press, 2007.

Martinez, Jared F. *The 10 Essentials of Forex Trading*. New York, NY: McGraw-Hill, 2007.

Page Harman, Hollis. *Money Sense for Kids*. Hauppauge, NY: Barron's Educational Series, 2005.

O'Keefe Ryan. *Making Money in Forex: Trade Like a Pro Without Giving Up Your Day Job*. Hoboken, NJ: John Wiley & Sons, Inc., 2010.

Schwager, Jack D. *Market Wizards: Interviews with Top Traders*. Columbia, MD: Marketplace Books, 2006.

Smith, Courtney. *How to Make a Living Trading Foreign Exchange: A Guaranteed Income for Life*. Hoboken, NJ: John Wiley & Sons, Inc., 2010.

# BIBLIOGRAPHY

BBC News. "Business: The Economy Brazil—a Catastrophe in the Making?" Retrieved January 2010 (http://news.bbc.co.uk/2/hi/business/260777.stm).

Beck, Frank. "Dollar Devaluation, the Final Frontier." Forbes.com, December 11, 2009. Retrieved January 2010 (http://www.forbes.com/2009/12/11/gold-dollar-commodities-personal-finance-financial-advisor-network-hard-assets.html).

Behravesh, Nariman. *Spin-Free Economics*. New York, NY: McGraw-Hill, 2009.

Berner, Richard. "2010 Outlook: From Exit to Exit." *Morgan Stanley: Global Economic Forum*. Retrieved December 2009 (http://www.morganstanley.com/views/gef/index.html).

Borensztein, Eduardo, and Jose De Gregorio. "Devaluation and Inflation After Currency Crisis." International Monetary Fund. Retrieved December 2009 (http://www.bcentral.cl/jdegrego/pdf/Bor-DeG%20PT_dev.pdf).

deCarbonnel, Eric. "Trade Deficits/Surpluses Around the World." Market Skeptics. Retrieved January 2010 (http://www.marketskeptics.com/2009/01/trade-deficitssurpluses-around-world.html).

E-commerce Journal. "Why Do Foreign Countries Compete in Currency Devaluation?" Retrieved December 2009 (http://www.ecommercejournal.com/articles/13974_why_do_foreign_countries_compete_in_currency_devaluation).

*The Economist. Guide to Economic Indicators, Making Sense of Economics.* New York, NY: Bloomberg Press, 2006.

Eichengreen, Barry. "Competitive Devaluation to the Rescue." Guardian.co.uk, March 17, 2009. Retrieved January 2010 (http://www.guardian.co.uk/commentisfree/2009/mar/17/g20-globalrecession).

Epping, Randy Charles. *The 21st-Century Economy—A Beginner's Guide.* New York, NY: Vintage Books.

Federal Reserve Bank of New York. "Currency Devaluation and Revaluation." Retrieved December 2009 (http://www.newyorkfed.org/aboutthefed/fedpoint/fed38.html).

FXStreet.com. "World Interest Rates Table." Retrieved December 2009 (http://www.fxstreet.com/fundamental/interest-rates-table).

International Monetary Fund. "The IMF's Response to the Asian Crisis." Factsheet, January 1999. Retrieved January 2010 (http://www.imf.org/external/np/exr/facts/asia.HTM).

Karmin, Craig. *Biography of the Dollar.* New York, NY: Three Rivers Press, 2009.

Rubino, John, and James Turk. *The Collapse of the Dollar and How to Profit from It.* New York, NY: Doubleday, 2004.

Thomson, Gale. "Beggar-Thy-Neighbor." International Encyclopedia of Social Sciences, 2008.Retrieved January 2010 (http://www.encyclopedia.com/doc/1G2-3045300173.html).

Twaronite, Lisa. "G20 Takes Aim at Currency Devaluation." MarketWatch. Retrieved January 2010 (http://www.marketwatch.com/story/g20-vow-make-nations-think-twice).

U.S. Census Bureau. "Foreign Trade." Retrieved December 2009 (http://www.census.gov/foreign-trade/index.html).

# INDEX

# About the Author

Barbara Gottfried Hollander has authored several economics and business books, including *How Credit Crises Happen*; *Money Matters: An Introduction to Economics*; *Booms, Bubbles, and Busts: The Economic Cycle*; *Managing Money*; *Raising Money*; and *Paying for College: Practical, Creative Strategies*. She is also the economics editor of the *World Almanac and Book of Facts*. Hollander received a B.A. in economics from the University of Michigan and an M.A. in economics from New York University, specializing in statistics and econometrics and international economics.

# Photo Credits

Cover (top), p. 1 (right) © www.istockphoto.com/Lilli Day; cover (bottom) Chris Thomaidis/Photographer's Choice/Getty Images; pp. 1 (left), 3, 4–5 © www.istockphoto.com/Dean Turner; p. 6 Robert Clare/ Photographer's Choice/Getty Images; pp. 8, 20, 30, 40, 51, 61 Mario Tama/Getty Images; p. 9 Shutterstock; pp. 12–13 Justin Sullivan/Getty Images; p. 15 Michael Lassman/Bloomberg via Getty Images; pp. 18–19 Tomohiro Ohsumi/Bloomberg via Getty Images; pp. 22–23 Tomohiro Ohsumi/AFP/Getty Images; pp. 24–25 Justin Sullivan/Getty Images; pp. 28–29 Roslan Rahman/AFP/Getty Images; p. 31 Jung Yeon-Je/AFP/ Getty Images; pp. 36–37 Jorge Uzon/AFP/Getty Images; pp. 38, 54–55, 62, 66 © AP Images; p. 41 Qilai Shen/Bloomberg via Getty Images; p. 45 Fabian Gredillas/AFP/Getty Images; p. 48 Daniel Garcia/AFP/ Getty Images; pp. 52–53 Mark Ralston/AFP/Getty Images; pp. 58–59 Hulton Archive/Archive Holdings, Inc./Getty Images; p. 65 Eric Feferberg/AFP/Getty Images; pp. 69, 71, 74, 76, 78 © www.istockphoto. com/studiovision.

Editor: Nicholas Croce; Photo Researcher: Marty Levick